Teeth and Eating

By the end of this book you will know more about:

- How animals feed.
- Balanced and varied diets.
- Different kinds of human teeth.
- How to keep teeth healthy.

You will:

- Use Fact Files, books, the Internet and CD-ROMs to help you answer questions.
- Do a survey.
- Make a bar chart.

Sealion

Giraffe

Elephant

Snake

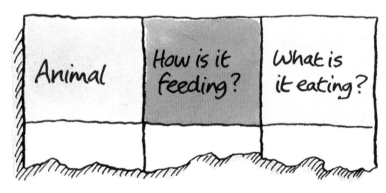

Butterfly

Task 1 How animals feed

When animals feed they take food into their bodies. Animals can feed by biting, drinking, chewing, sucking, filtering food or swallowing it whole.

✸ How are the animals feeding in the photographs?

✸ What are they eating?
Copy this table. Fill it in.

Animal	How is it feeding?	What is it eating?

Extra Challenge

✸ Use books or CD-ROMs to find out how some other animals feed.

✸ Add them to your table.

How did you feed yesterday?

 Write down what you ate and drank yesterday.

List the foods and drinks in a table and describe how you got each food into your body.

Food	Way of feeding
Breakfast	
Cornflakes	chewing
milk	drinking
toast	biting and chewing

Look at your finished table.

- Which was your most common way of feeding?
- Which was your least common way of feeding?

> **Words to learn and use:**
> feed
> feeding
> filtering
> swallowing

Fact File

Food and oxygen

- Food changes as it goes through our bodies.

- Most food goes into the blood.

- The blood takes food to all parts of our bodies, including our muscles.

- The oxygen we breathe in is also taken to our muscles.

- The food and oxygen together give us energy. This energy helps us to move.

The head of a blue whale

How the blue whale feeds

- The blue whale is the largest creature on Earth.
- Blue whales can grow 30 metres long. They can weigh 150-200 tonnes. That's as heavy as about 35 African elephants.
- They feed on krill. Krill are small pinkish animals like shrimps.
- There are about 600 billion krill in the Southern Ocean, where most blue whales live.
- A blue whale has two rows of horny filters hanging from the roof of its mouth.
- These filters trap the krill in the blue whale's mouth.
- A blue whale eats about 6 million krill a day.

All animals need to feed to grow and to be active.

Task 3

Why do we need to eat?

The teacher of Class 3 asked:
Why do we need to eat?

Here are some of their ideas.

So that we have good teeth and skin.

So that we grow.

To help us grow into a bigger person.

To give us energy to do things.

To help us to run.

Some foods help us to see in the dark.

 In your group, write down some of your own ideas about why we need to eat.

Groups of foods

People need to eat a range of different kinds of foods. Look at the picture showing lots of foods.

 How many foods can you name?

 We can sort foods into groups. How would you sort the foods in the picture? By colour? Shape? Taste? Favourites?

Scientists group foods into those we need for our bodies to **grow** and those we need for us to be **active**.

We need **meat, fish, lentils and beans, milk** and things made from **milk** for our bodies to grow.

Sugars and starches give us energy to be active. We get them from foods such as bread and potatoes. **Fats** - found in foods like cheese, butter, and some meats - also give us energy.

Food for activity	Food for growth

 Look at the picture and make a list of some foods needed for growth and some foods needed for activity.

Eating well keeps you healthy.

Food from around the world

We usually have plenty of food to eat in Britain, but we do not grow all of it in this country. You can buy a wide range of fresh fruits and vegetables in a supermarket all the year round. Some of these have to be imported from other countries. Some food is frozen or stored in cans so that we can eat it at any time of year.

- Look at the picture of fruits and vegetables. How many can you name?

- Use books, CD-ROMs and the Internet to find out which countries the fruits might have come from.

- Make a table like this.

- Complete Task Sheet 1.

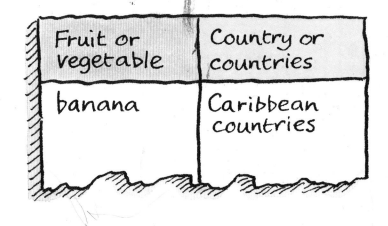

Fruit or vegetable	Country or countries
banana	Caribbean countries

 Task 6

Food labels

- Collect some labels from boxes, packets and tins of food.

  - Which country does each package come from?

  - List the foods they contain.

  - Which foods are for activity and which for growth? Make a table.

Task 7 Meals from around the world

Asian meal

European meal

Look at the pictures showing a meal from Asia and a meal from Europe.

- How many foods can you name?

- What types of food are they?

- Copy the table and record them.

European meal	Type of food
chips fish bread and butter baked beans strawberries/cream	active growth
Asian meal	
chicken curry rice nan lentils gulab jaman	

Healthy eating

2,3

Everything we eat is called our diet.
Everyone needs a **balanced diet**. It
includes all the things you need to
grow, to be active and to keep healthy.

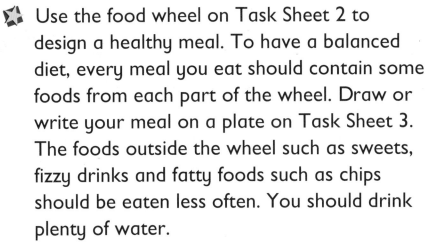

✴ Use the food wheel on Task Sheet 2 to
design a healthy meal. To have a balanced
diet, every meal you eat should contain some
foods from each part of the wheel. Draw or
write your meal on a plate on Task Sheet 3.
The foods outside the wheel such as sweets,
fizzy drinks and fatty foods such as chips
should be eaten less often. You should drink
plenty of water.

Extra Challenge

✴ Make a different menu for
two of these people:

- an active adult

- a growing teenager

- an athlete

- you.

**Different animals have different diets.
Make a bar chart.**

Task **9** *What do our pets eat?*

The teacher of Class 3 asked:
How could you find out what your pets eat?

Here are some of the children's ideas.

Let's
watch them eat a
choice of food.

We could read about
their diet in a book.

Use a computer
and CD-ROM.

Let's
write the names of the
foods each of the pets eat
in a day.

I could read the
label on the tins with
my mum.

✦ Think of some questions your group
could research. Write them down.

✦ Now try to find the answers to
your questions.
Think about what you will use to
find your answers.

✦ Share your questions and answers
with the rest of the class.

Scientific Enquiry
Do all pets eat the same food?

`4,5`

Class 3 decided to investigate the question: *Do all pets eat the same food?*

They did a class survey using a survey planning board to help them.

- Get into groups to investigate your own question by doing a survey. Use the survey planning board on Task Sheet 4 to make your plan.

- Talk about how you will do your survey. Carry out your survey and add each person's findings to the table.

- Your teacher will help to make a class table of all the results for the class.

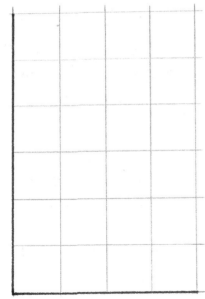

number of pets

type of food

- Try making your table into a bar chart using Task Sheet 5.

- Look at your bar chart. Use these questions to help you understand it. Try to answer them as a group.

  - How many pets did you use in the survey?

  - Did the pets eat the same food?

  - Which foods were fed to the pets?

  - Which foods did the pets like most? Least? How do you know?

Animals have different kinds of teeth.

Different types of TEETH

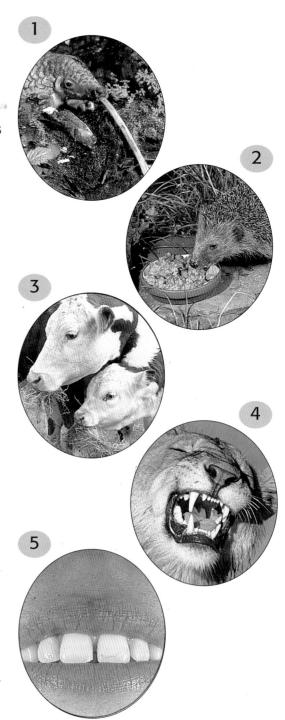

Fact File

Humans and some other animals use their teeth for feeding. Their teeth come in many shapes and sizes. Different kinds of teeth do different jobs. Some animals don't have any teeth and feed in other ways.

1. The pangolin does not have proper teeth. It eats ants and termites with its long, sticky tongue. It crushes its food in its stomach.

2. A hedgehog has small, very sharp teeth to chew grubs, worms and beetles.

3. A cow has broad flat teeth for grinding grass. It has no top teeth at the front. Its bottom front teeth are sharp and cut the grass on the upper gum, like a knife on a chopping board.

4. A lion's mouth has huge, sharp pointed teeth at the side for capturing and killing animals. Its back teeth are like scissors. They cut flesh into smaller lumps for swallowing.

5. Humans have front sharp teeth called **incisors**. They are used for biting food. Pointed side teeth called **canines** tear food. At the back, flat-topped **premolar** and **molar** teeth grind and chew food.

Gums are quite soft and pink. They cover and help to protect the jaw bones. If the gums are unhealthy the jaw bones may become unhealthy too, and teeth can fall out.

Animals and their teeth

✪ Read the Fact File on page 12.

✪ Talk about what each animal eats. What kind of teeth do you think each animal needs?

✪ What type of teeth do humans have?

✪ Make a table like this.

Animal	Type of teeth

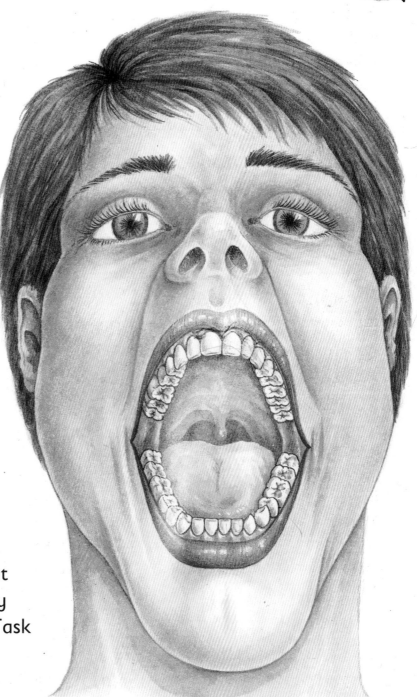

✪ Look at the picture. Can you spot the different kinds of teeth in the adult's mouth?

✪ How many kinds of teeth can you see?

✪ What does each kind do?

✪ Why are they suited to this job?

✪ Read the Fact File to find out about human teeth and copy and complete the table on Task Sheet 6.

Observe and compare different teeth.

 Task 12 _Using dental records_

When you have your teeth checked, the dentist always makes a record of what your teeth are like. Using a special mirror like this one, the dentist can see if your teeth and gums are healthy. The dental nurse fills in your dental record.

Look at Paul Jones' dental record on Task Sheet 7.

In your group, talk about the dental record, using the following questions:

- How many teeth have been filled?

- What was wrong with upper left 5?

- Which tooth has been taken out?

- Which teeth will the dentist have to fill?

A dental mirror

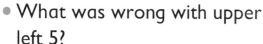

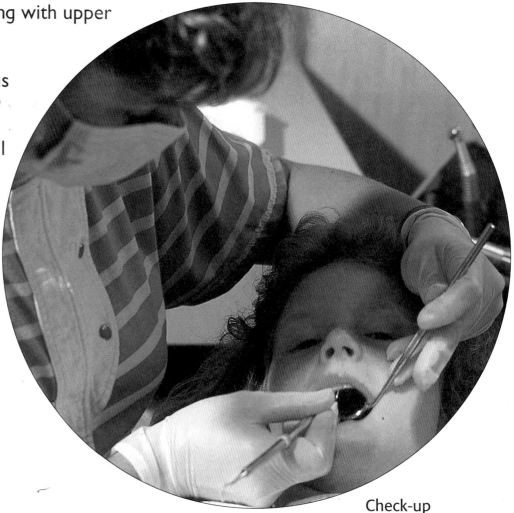

Check-up

You have two sets of teeth in your lifetime.

Milk teeth

A baby lives mostly on a diet of milk and usually has no teeth. After a while teeth start to grow. By the age of six, a child may have their first set of teeth. These are called milk teeth.

Milk teeth taken from a six-year-old child. The long roots anchor the teeth in the jaws.

⚡ Look at the picture. How many kinds of teeth can you see? Name them.

⚡ How many incisors, canines and premolars can you count?

⚡ How many of each kind are there in a full set of milk teeth?

⚡ Cut out the teeth on Task Sheet 8 and stick them in their correct place in the child's lower jaw.

> **Words to learn and use:**
> canine
> decay
> incisor
> milk teeth
> molar
> permanent teeth
> premolar

Jim aged 6

Jim aged 12

Jim aged 25

The milk teeth are replaced by permanent teeth. The permanent teeth are your last set of real teeth (they do not get replaced).

Look at the pictures of Jim. He still had his milk teeth when he was fully grown. Why do you think we need two sets of teeth?

You may have some permanent teeth already. When you are about 18 you may have all your teeth. In a full adult set, there are four incisors, 2 canines, 4 premolars and 6 molars in each jaw.

How many teeth are there in an adult's top jaw?

How many teeth are there in an adult's lower jaw?

Finish off the cartoon story on Task Sheet 9 by drawing what happens when a child loses a milk tooth.

Finish off the cartoon story on Task Sheet 9 by drawing what happens when an adult loses a tooth.

Which story has the happier ending?

My dental record

10

Using a very clean dental or plastic mirror, take turns with a partner to look at each other's teeth. Use Task Sheet 10 to make your partner's dental record. Swap dental records.

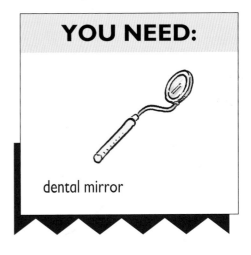

YOU NEED:

dental mirror

⚠ *Clean the mirror each time you use it.*

✳ How many teeth do you have in your bottom jaw? In your top jaw?

✳ How many have become diseased and have fillings?

✳ How many milk teeth have you lost?

✳ How many permanent teeth are there?

✳ How many have still to appear?

What is a tooth made of?

Each of our teeth has a hard white coat called **enamel**.

Below the gum, the root of the tooth has a covering. This is called the **cement**. It fixes the tooth to the jaw bone.

Underneath the enamel is **dentine**. It is not as hard as enamel.

In the centre of the tooth is the **pulp cavity**. This contains blood vessels and nerves. The blood brings food and oxygen to the living parts of the tooth. The nerves feel pain, especially when a tooth decays.

Gums are pink and cover the jaw bones. They protect the bone and help to stop teeth becoming wobbly and falling out.

If food is trapped on teeth, tiny living things called **bacteria** can feed on it. A thin layer of bacteria can form on teeth and gums. This is called **plaque**. Plaque can cause enamel to decay and then gums become diseased.

Task 6 *What is a tooth made of?*

 Use the information in the Fact File and the diagram to copy and complete this table.

Part of tooth	Description
enamel	
	found underneath the enamel
pulp cavity	
	fixes the tooth to the jaw bone
	pink, cover the jaw bone

Inside a tooth

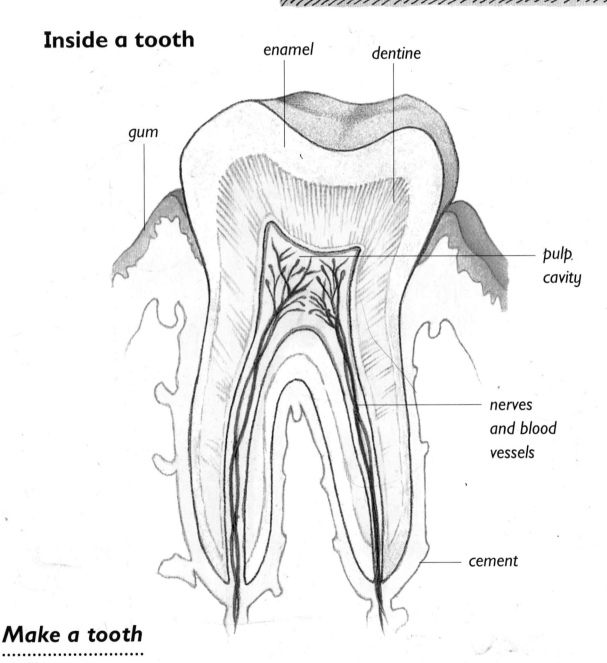

enamel

dentine

gum

pulp cavity

nerves and blood vessels

cement

Task 17 *Make a tooth*

11

 Use Task Sheet 11 to make a model of a tooth.

 What kind of tooth is your model?

Some foods can harm your teeth.

Task **18** *Looking after our teeth*

We can help stop tooth decay by:

- Visiting the dentist at least twice a year for a check-up.

- Cleaning teeth after meals and **especially before going to bed**.

- Using a fluoride toothpaste.

- Eating sweets and drinking sugary drinks only after meals – not between meals.

- Eating more fresh fruit and raw vegetables as snacks.

- Drinking water after meals to rinse food from teeth and gums.

- Brushing back teeth and gums gently as scrubbing can damage gums. Using a scrubbing action on insisors.

Some dentists tell you to clean your tongue with toothpaste. Do you know why?

Class 3 did a survey to find out how children look after their teeth.

✦ Look at the table. This shows you how 30 children in Class 3 look after their teeth.

✦ How many children in Class 3 clean their teeth before going to bed?

✦ How many children use a fluoride toothpaste?

✦ How many visit the dentist twice a year?

✦ How many do not use fluoride toothpaste?

✦ Which of the things do you do? Make a list.

What Class 3 do to look after their teeth?	How many children do this in Class 3?
Eat fruit and vegetables every day.	10
Clean teeth after meals and before going to bed.	25
Only eat sweets straight after a meal.	2
Drink water with a meal.	5
Clean their teeth with a flouride toothpaste.	20
Visit the dentist twice a year.	24
Drink more milk and less pop.	7

Watch what you eat

⊠ Sort these foods into two groups – those
that are likely to harm teeth and those that
are less likely to harm teeth. Make a table.

Foods likely to harm teeth	Foods that are less harmful to teeth

⊠ Ask other people to sort the foods into
groups like you did. How good are they at
this? Do you need to help them?

Checkpoint 1

The Back Teeth Gang

✻ Write a story for young children about teeth.

✻ Some things to think about:

- How will you research your story?

- What will you need to find out?

- How could you use what you have learned about teeth?

- How will your story help the children to learn about teeth?

Checkpoint 2

Fact cards

✻ Design and make fact cards about teeth and eating.

Fact card 1 should include facts about different kinds of teeth, what they are used for and how to care for teeth and gums.

Fact card 2 should show some ways of eating a varied but balanced diet. It should also show balanced diets from other cultures.

Summary

Which of these do you know and which can you do?

- I know that all animals need to feed to grow and to be active.
- I know that eating well keeps you healthy.
- I know that different animals have different diets.
- I know that animals have different kinds of teeth.
- I know that you have two sets of teeth in your lifetime.
- I know that healthy teeth need healthy gums.
- I know that some foods can harm your teeth.
- I can make a bar chart.
- I can observe and compare teeth.

Complete your **Science Log** to show how well you know these and how well you can do them. Circle a face for each statement.

Glossary

canine

balanced diet - all the things we need to eat to grow, be active and healthy.

canine - a tooth at the side of the mouth which tears and shreds food.

cement - the covering of a root which holds a tooth firmly in the jaw.

decay - to rot away.

dentine - the soft layer inside a tooth underneath the enamel.

enamel - the hard covering of a tooth.

feed - to take food into the body by chewing, drinking etc.

gum - soft, pink covering of the jaw bones.

incisor - a tooth at the front of the mouth which bites and cuts food.

jaws - the bones of the head in which the teeth are anchored.

molar - a tooth at the back of the mouth which helps to crush and grind food.

plaque - a sort of white fur that can damage teeth.

premolar - a grinding tooth between the canines and molars.

pulp cavity - the part inside a tooth which contains blood vessels and nerves.

root - the bottom part of a tooth which is anchored in the jaw.

sugars and starches - chemicals found in potatoes, cereals and other foods that give us energy.

sugars

starches